Like all birds

Christian Merveille
illustrated by : Emma de Woot

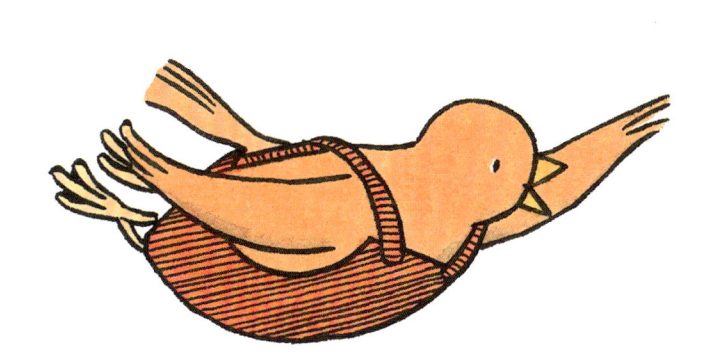

JYOTSNA PRAKASHAN

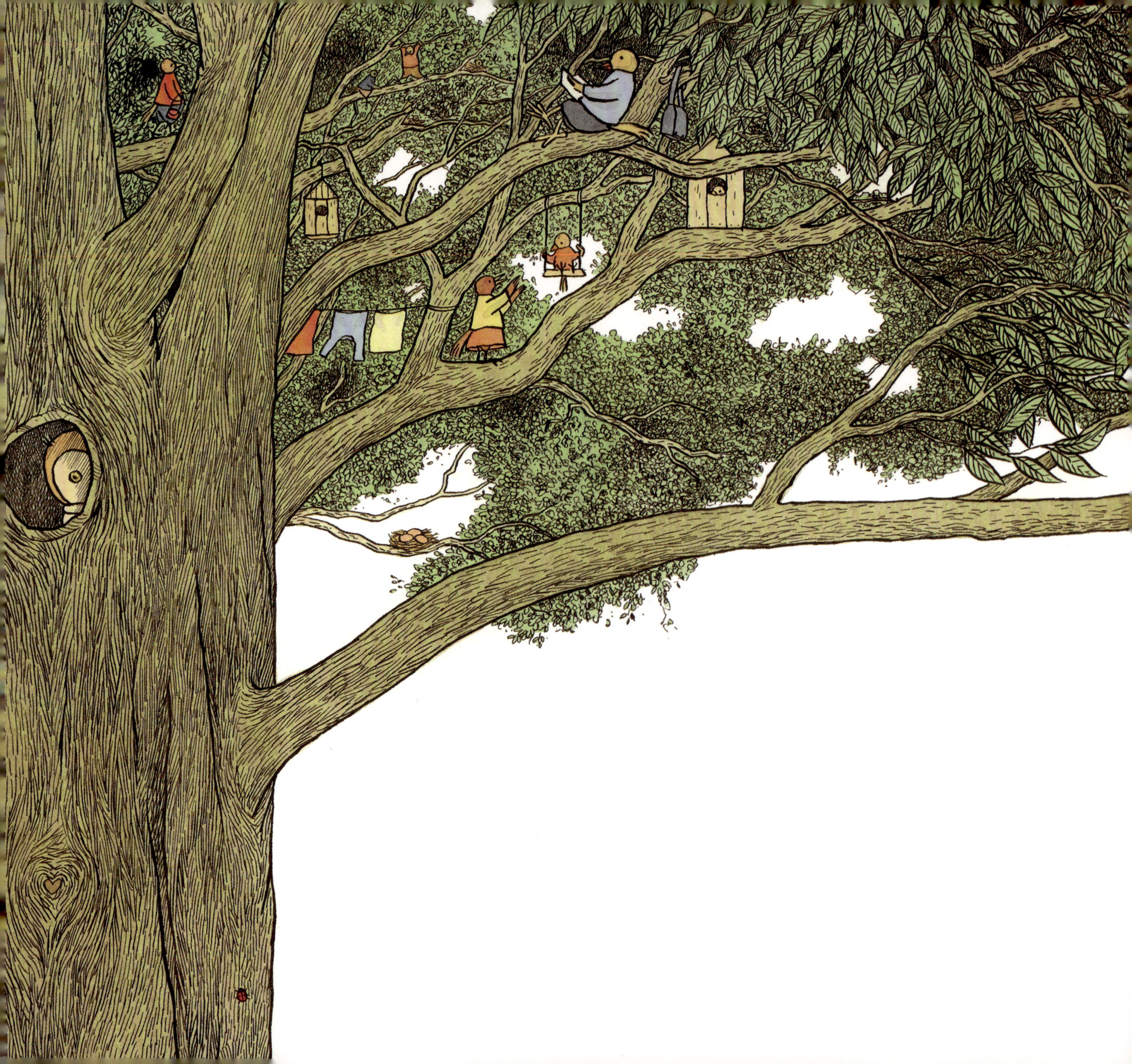

Little Bird is worried : he feels he is too small
and he is bored in his nest. 'My life is so miserable here.
I want to explore the world, and discover how others live....'

'That's it, I am leaving!
Watch out, don't fall!'

A mouse is amused by this.
'Will he fall? Won't he fall?'
It is the very first time
he sees a bird
come down a tree this way!

"Hey you, who are you?" asks Little Bird. "I do not know you."
"I am the mouse, and you?"
"I am Little Bird. I left my nest.
I want to explore the world, and discover how others live...
And you, what is your life like?"

"Me," says the mouse,
"I live the life of a mouse.
I slip under the leaves,
I sleep with one eye open,
I am wary of everything,
and I curl up in my little hole."

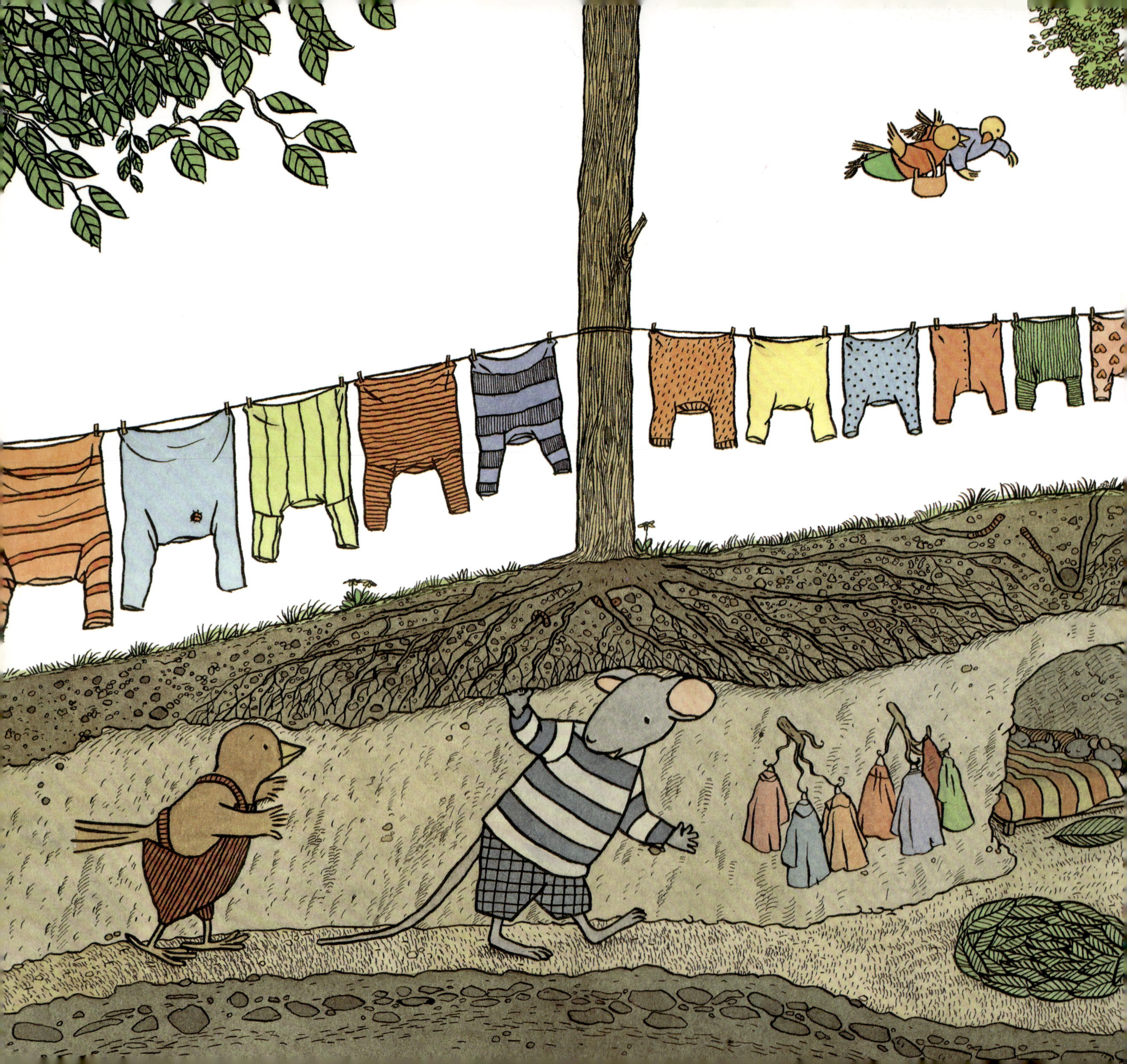

"Ah," says Little Bird,
"It is true that where you live is not high enough!
You must all bump into each other in your hole,
and you have to feel your way inside it. It is wierd, your house..."
"I have told you," replied the mouse.
"It is a house of mice and this is how I live!"

"Thank you," says Little Bird.
"Your place is too small.
I don't think I can live the life of a mouse.
We will probably meet again by chance.
Thank you for everything. It was good,
but I think I will go further to see more...."

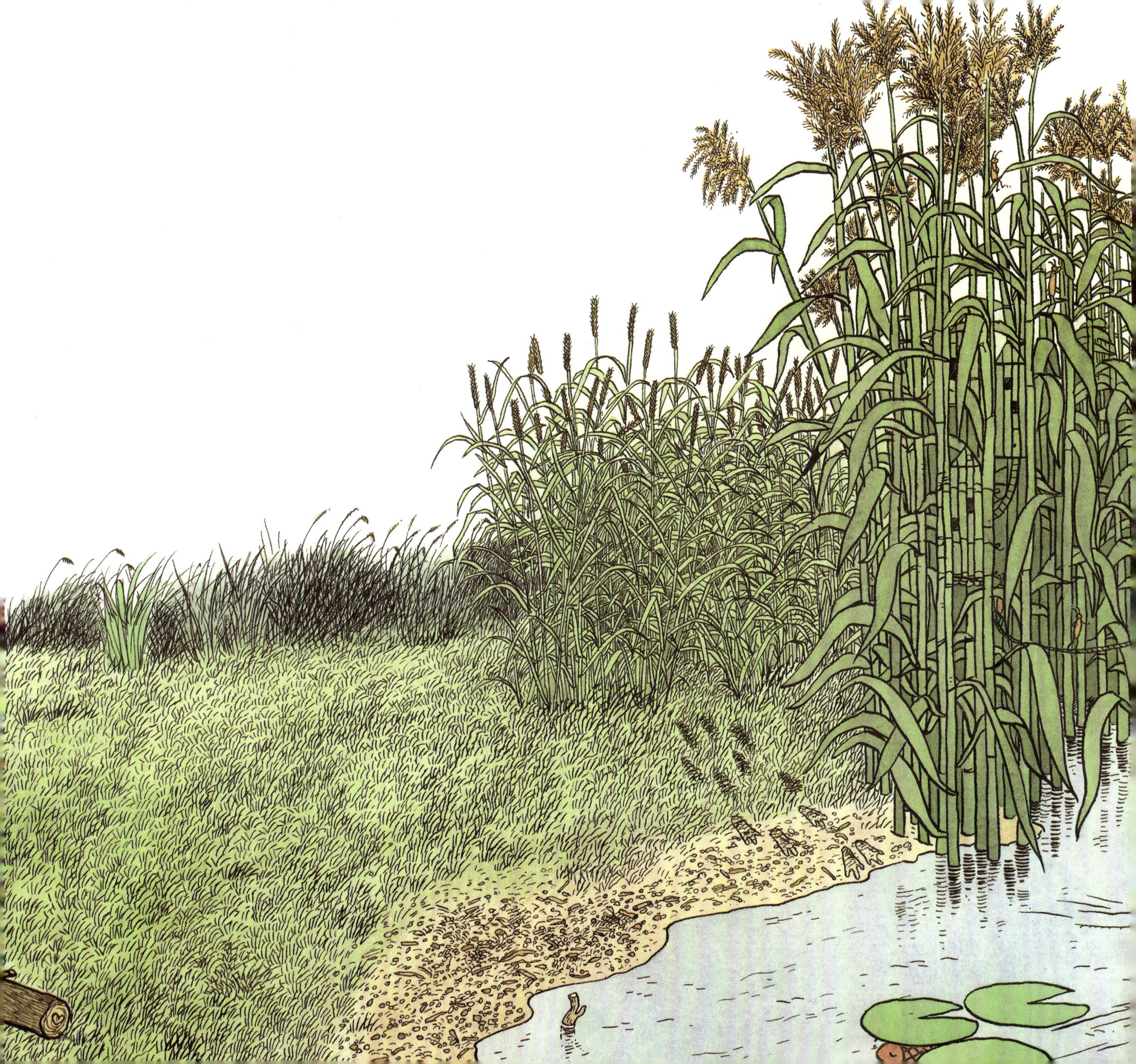

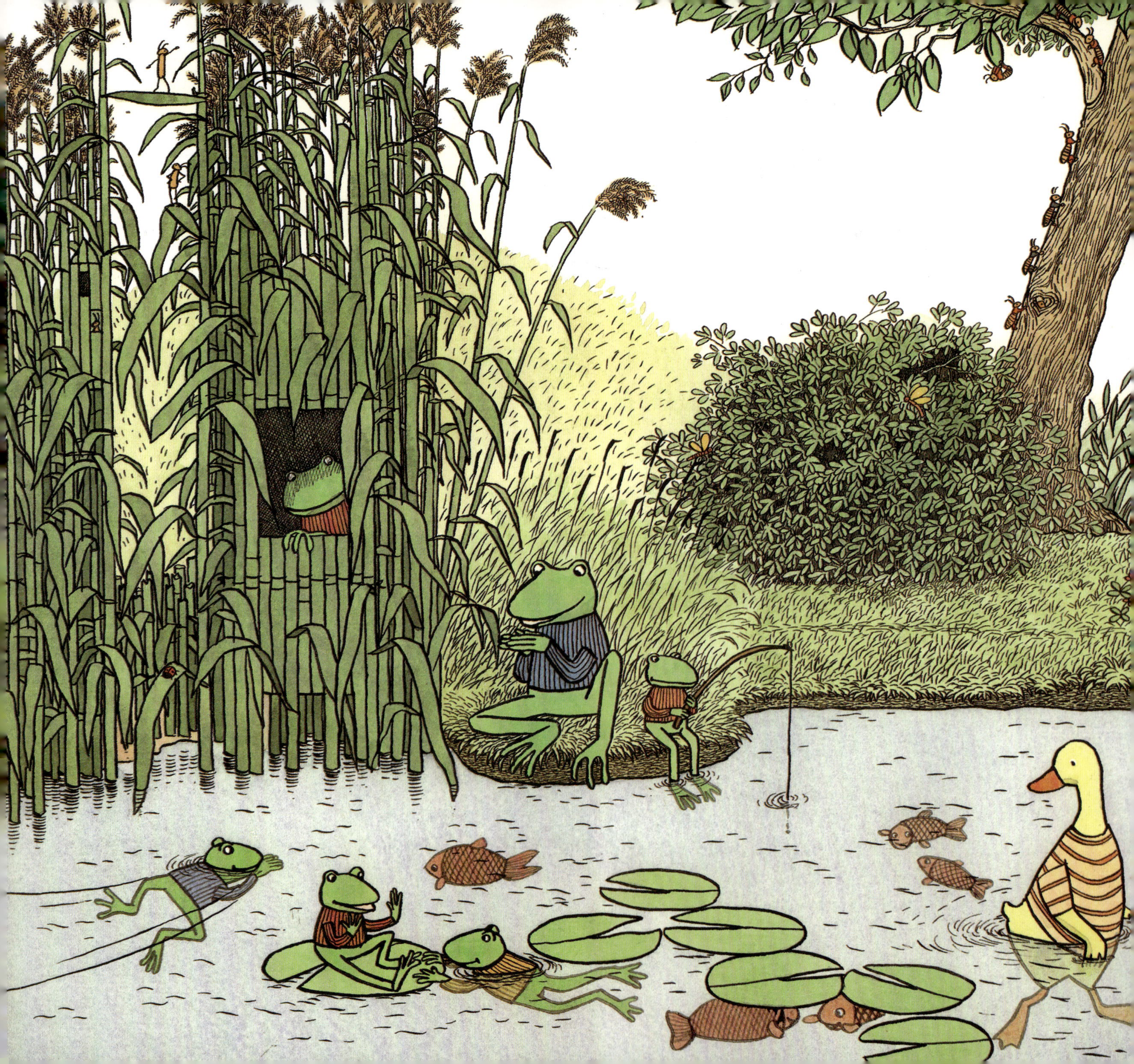

"Hey you, who are you?" asks Little Bird. "I do not know you."
"I am the duck, and you?"
"I am Little Bird. I left my nest.
I want to explore the world, and discover how others live...
And you, what is your life like?"
"Me," says the duck, "I live in the pond.
I dive, I swim... just like all ducks!"

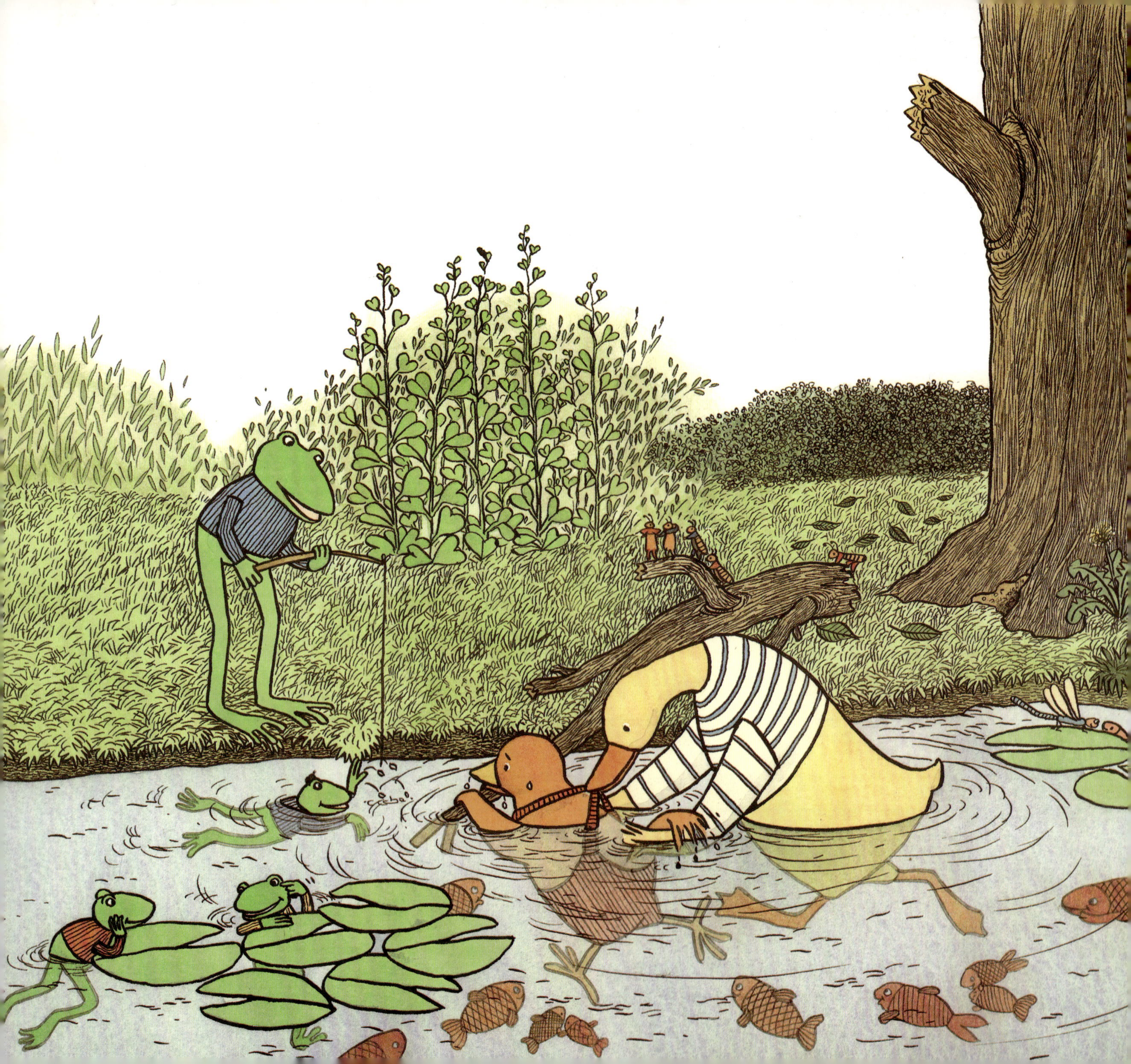

"Ahhh! I can't swim!" cries Little Bird.
"I am going to drown..."
Laughing, the duck helps out Little Bird,
who thinks he can't live the life of a duck,
even though he has feathers, and he is a bird,
he is not made for swimming,
he has to go further away to find the life that suits him.

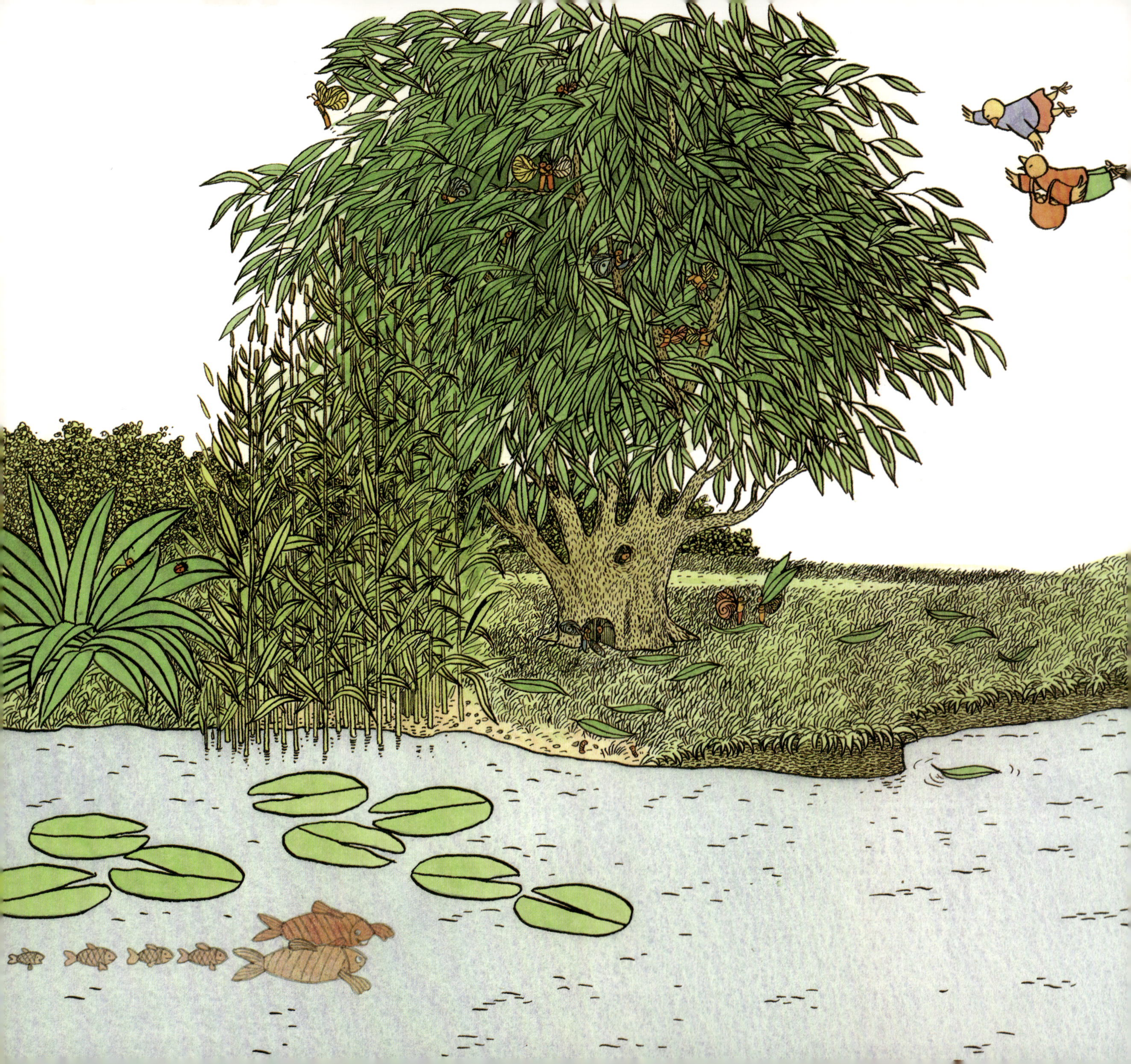

Little Bird is tired.
Little Bird is discouraged.
He was almost going to drown...
Shall he stop?
Shall he continue?
Where shall he go?
Suddenly, a dog starts barking
from behind the fence.

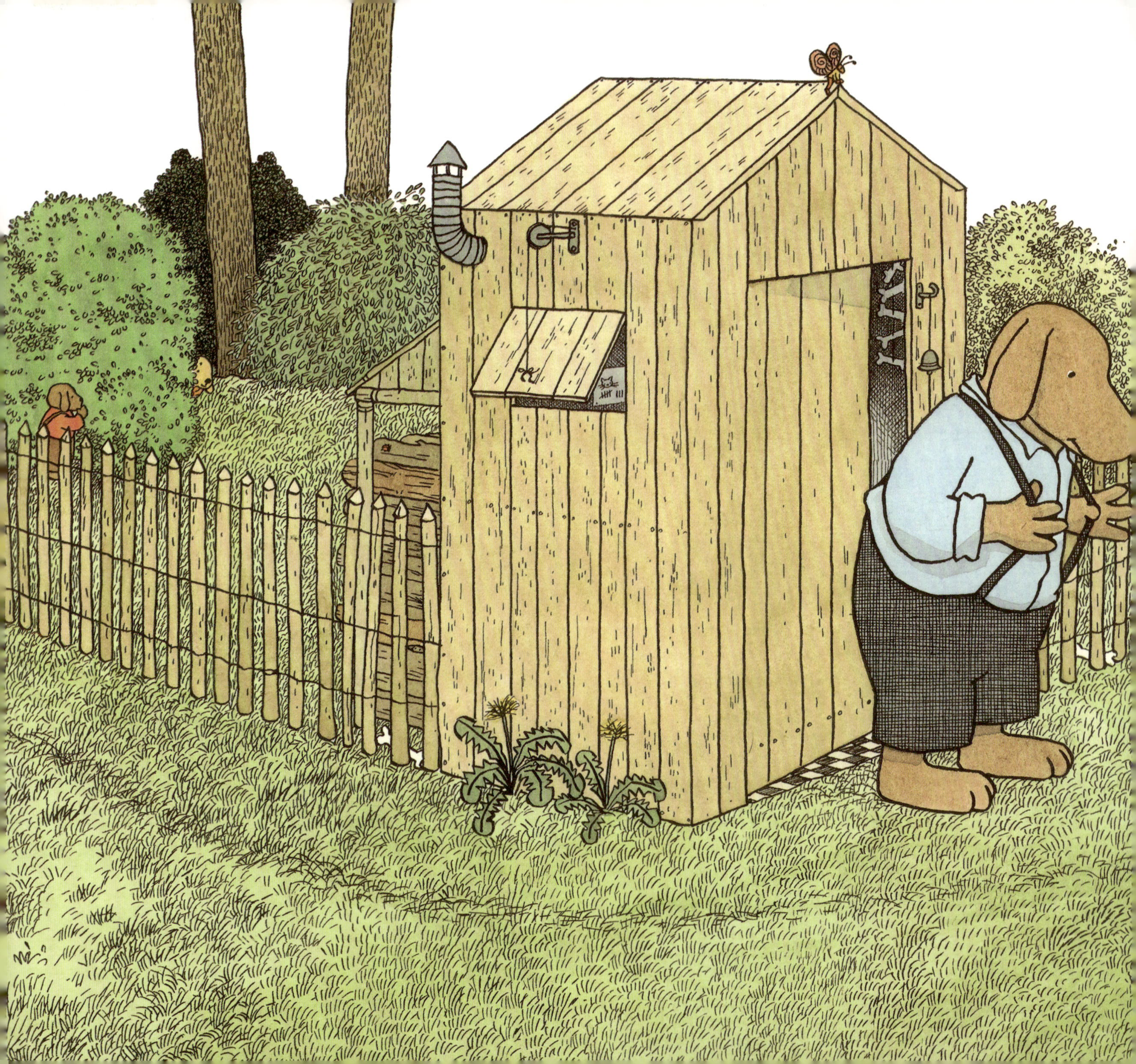

"Who are you?" asks Little Bird. "I do not know you."
"I am the dog, and you?"
"I am Little Bird. I left my nest.
I want to explore the world, and discover how others live...
And you, what is your life like?"
"Me," says the dog, "I live the life of a dog : I sleep outdoors,
I guard the house, and I bark on the slightest occasion...."

"Woof! Woof!" suddenly yells the dog,
And with a quick leap, he bounds in pursuit of a cat passing by.
"I can't stand this cat!
At home he gets all the attention.
They spoil him, but never me."
'That doesn't mean I should be knocked down!'
thinks Little Bird, 'This dog was about to crush me....'

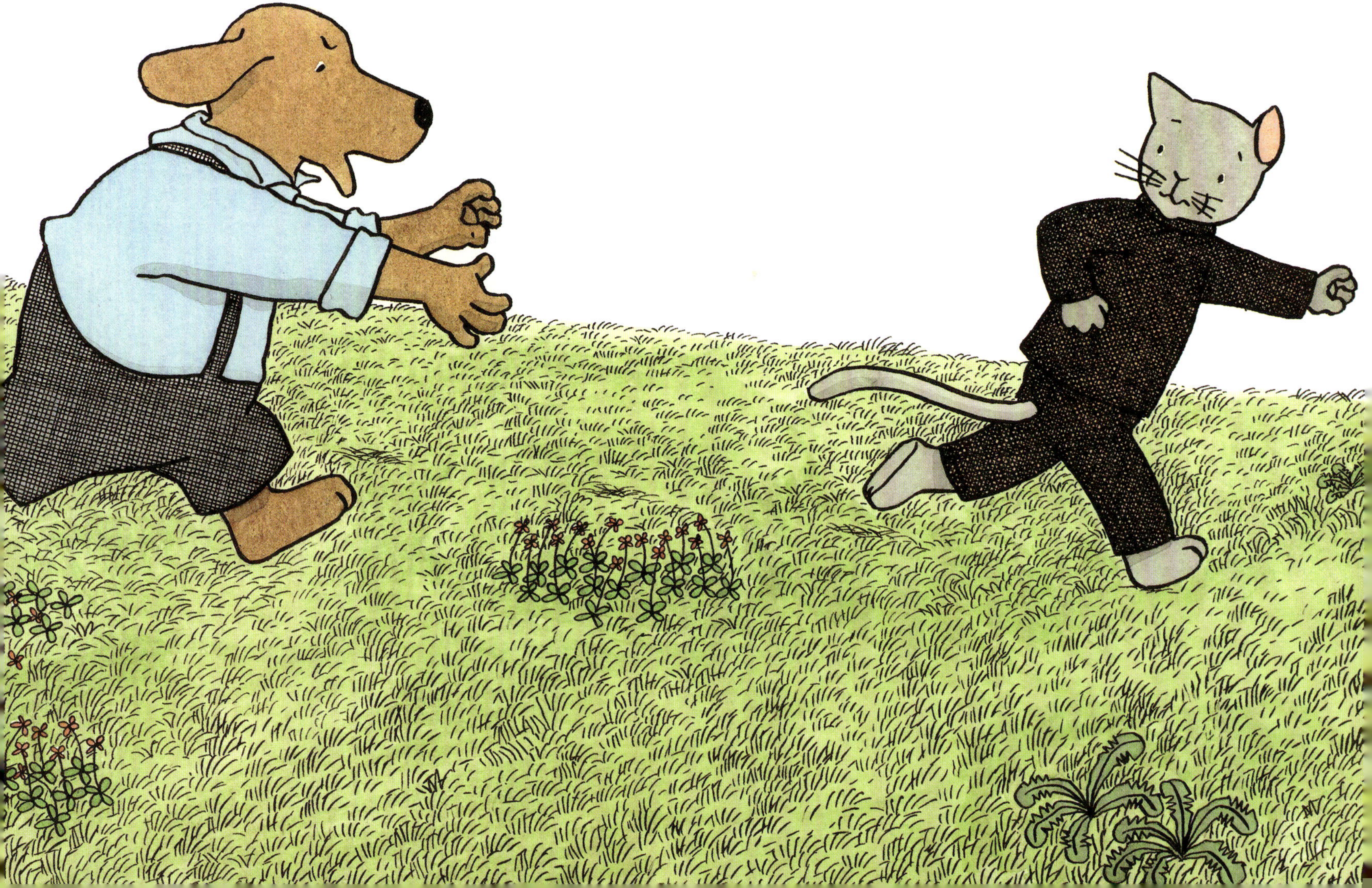

'I will actually stay away from this cat myself!
And from the dog too.
Hurry, hurry, I am out of here!'
Little Bird runs off. He runs and runs,
as fast as his little feet can take him,
and suddenly to his surprise, he starts flying....

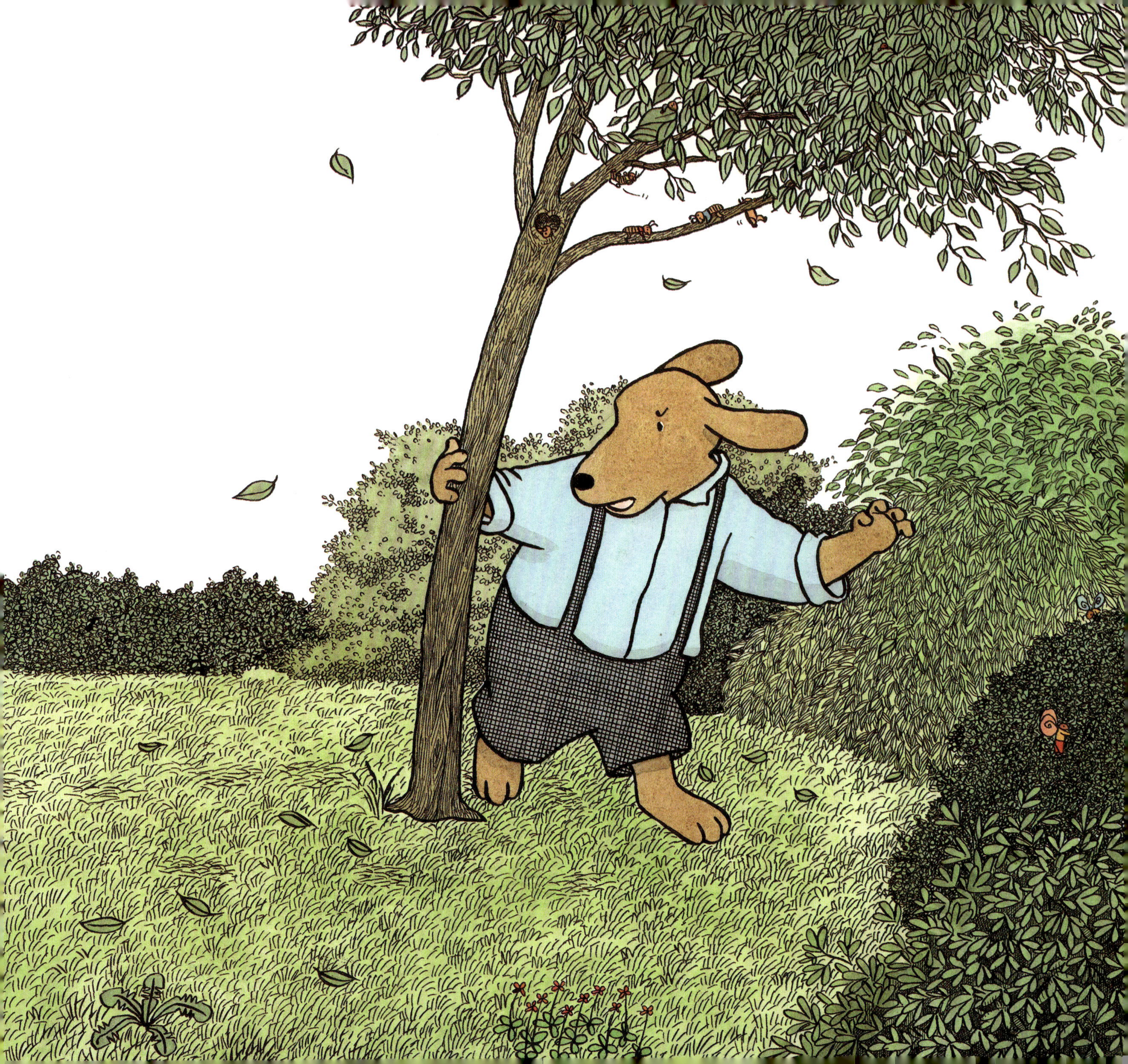

Little Bird is a bird
and, like all birds,
Little Bird flies.
That's it, the life of a bird!